LAURA K. MURRAY

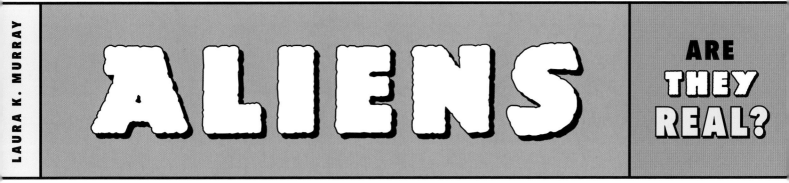

ALIENS

ARE THEY REAL?

CREATIVE EDUCATION · CREATIVE PAPERBACKS

Published by Creative Education and Creative Paperbacks
P.O. Box 227, Mankato, Minnesota 56002
Creative Education and Creative Paperbacks are imprints of The Creative Company
www.thecreativecompany.us

Design and production by **Christine Vanderbeek**
Art direction by **Rita Marshall**
Printed in the United States of America

Photographs by Alamy (AF archive, ZUMA Press Inc.), Corbis (Bettmann, Science Photo Library, Norbert Wu/Minden Pictures), Dreamstime (1971yes, Chorazin3d, Kitkana, Julien Tromeur), NASA (NASA/ESA; NASA/JPL-Caltech; NASA/JPL-Caltech/STScI; NASA, ESA, and the Hubble Heritage Team [STScI/AURA]-ESA/Hubble Collaboration), Shutterstock (M. Cornelius, Dragan85, EKS, Fer Gregory, Chris Harvey, Lena_graphics, Nejron Photo, photoBeard, razum, solarseven, Top Photo Corporation)

Library of Congress Cataloging-in-Publication Data
Murray, Laura K. Aliens / Laura K. Murray. p. cm. – (Are they real?) Includes index. Summary: A high-interest inquiry into the possible existence of aliens, emphasizing reported sightings and stories as well as scientific investigations and unsolved mysteries.

ISBN 978-1-60818-759-1 (hardcover) **ISBN 978-1-62832-367-2** (pbk) **ISBN 978-1-56660-801-5** (ebook)
1. Extraterrestrial beings–Juvenile literature. 2. Human-alien encounters–Juvenile literature. 3. Life on other planets–Juvenile literature.
QB54.M867 2017
001.942–dc23   2016008265

CCSS: RI.1.1, 2, 4, 5, 6, 7, 10; RI.2.1, 2, 4, 5, 6, 7; RI.3.1, 2, 5, 6, 7; RF.1.1, 2, 3, 4; RF.2.3, 4; RF.3.3, 4

First Edition HC 9 8 7 6 5 4 3 2 1   **First Edition PBK** 9 8 7 6 5 4 3 2 1

CONTENTS

A BRIGHT LIGHT

Betty and Barney Hill are driving home. The road is dark and quiet. What is that bright light? It looks like a ship from outer space.

LITTLE GRAY CREATURES ARE INSIDE!

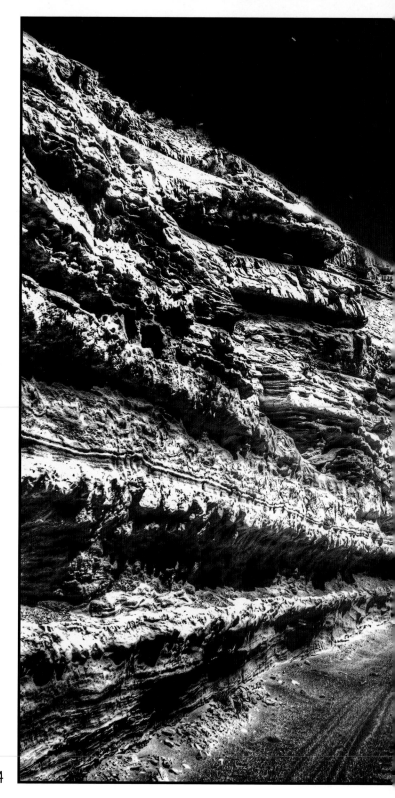

ALIEN VISITORS

STARS AND PLANETS FORM IN CLOUDS OF GAS AND DUST.

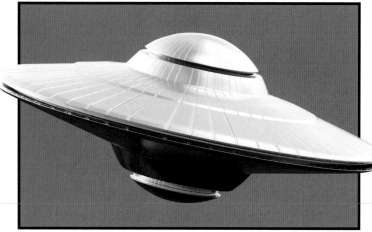

Aliens are creatures from other **PLANETS** or worlds. Some people say aliens visit Earth. They say **UFOs** fly through the sky. Others do not think aliens are real.

SOME PEOPLE THINK UFOs HAVE CRASHED ON EARTH.

WHAT DO ALIENS LOOK LIKE?

Some aliens may have gray skin.

Their huge heads could have big brains inside. They have big, dark eyes.

Other aliens may look like lizards, sea animals, or even humans!

WHAT DO ALIENS DO?

Aliens are smart. They want to learn about human life. They may be able to read your thoughts!

ALIENS MIGHT COME FROM FARAWAY PARTS OF SPACE.

Some people say they have been on alien ships. Were they dreaming?

SCIENTISTS have not found aliens yet. But they listen for messages from space. They use powerful TELESCOPES. They look for new planets.

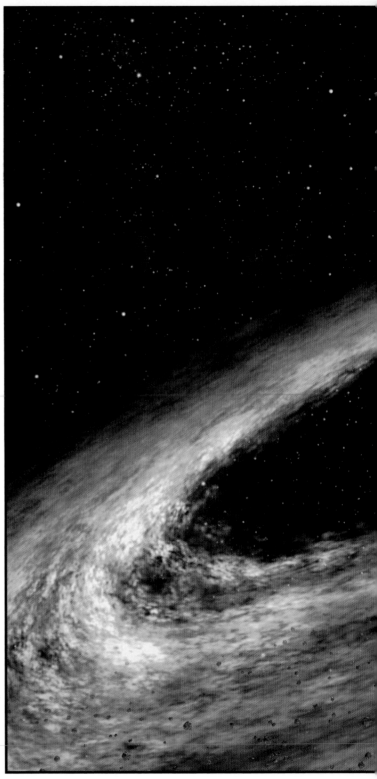

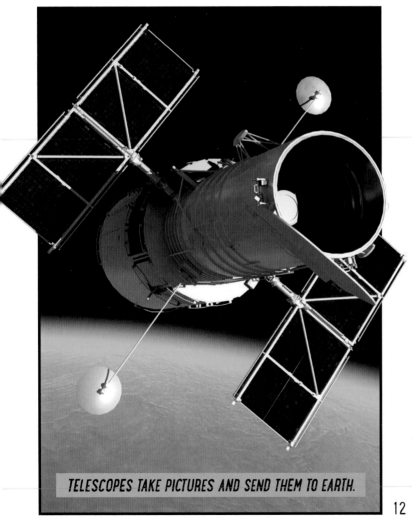

TELESCOPES TAKE PICTURES AND SEND THEM TO EARTH.

12

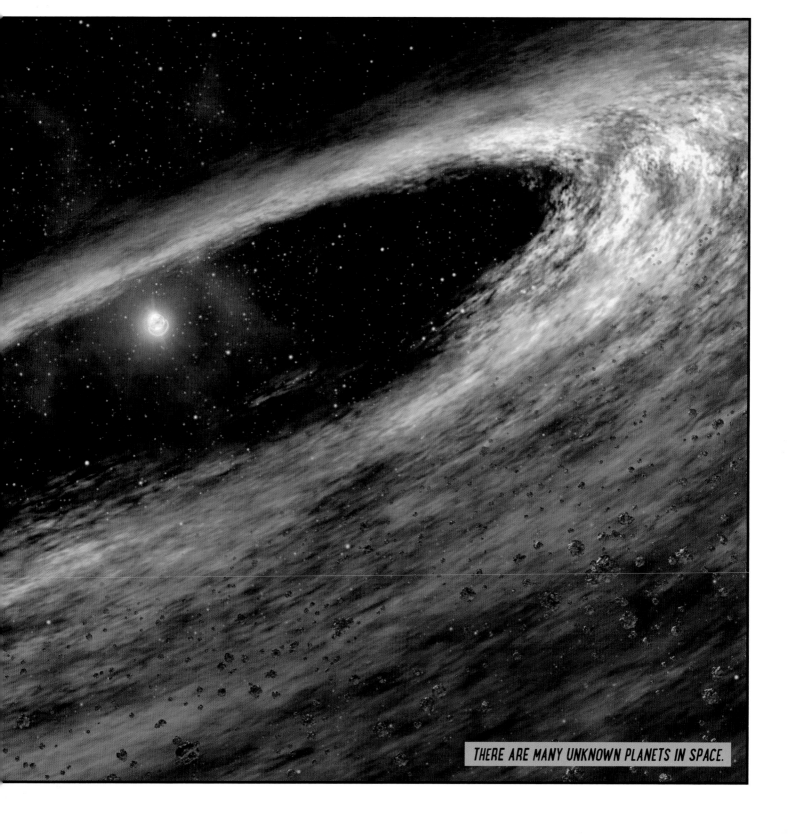

THERE ARE MANY UNKNOWN PLANETS IN SPACE.

STORIES OF ALIENS

In 1947, a flying object crashed near Roswell, New Mexico. Some people said it was a UFO with aliens.

The government said it was a **WEATHER BALLOON.** Who was right?

It can be fun to read about aliens in **SCI-FI** books. Movies like *E.T.: The Extra-Terrestrial*

and *Lilo and Stitch* have friendly aliens! Comic books and video games have aliens, too.

17

ALIEN ENCOUNTERS

Real aliens could be very different from what we think. Stephen Hawking and other scientists want to find out. They look for life in outer space. There are many places to explore!

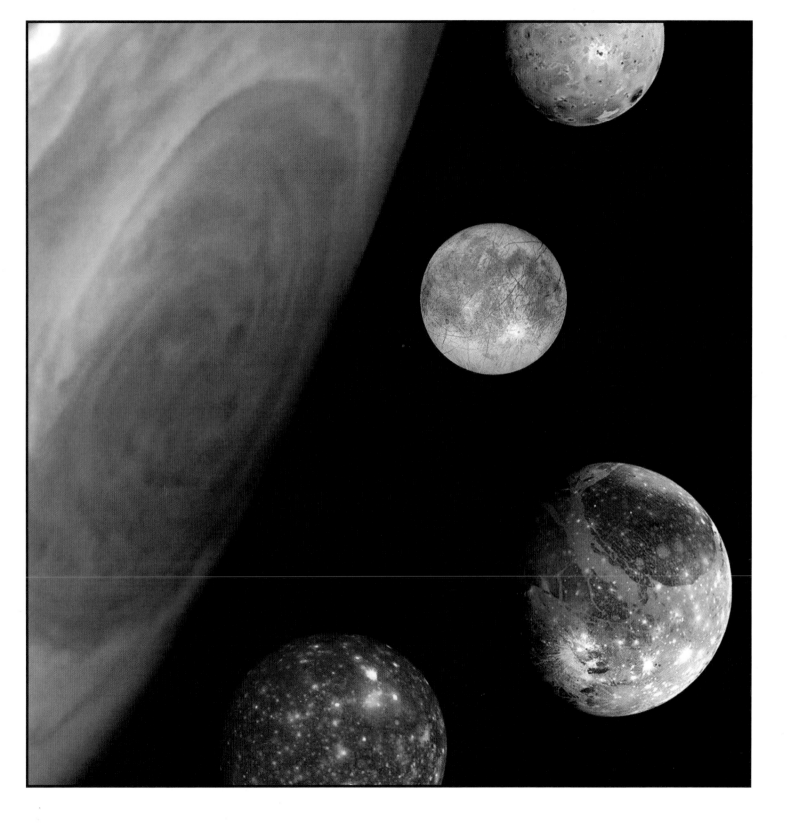

What would you do if you saw an alien?

SEE IF THE ALIEN CAN READ YOUR THOUGHTS!

INVESTIGATE IT!
EXPLORE THE SKY

Go outside on a clear night. Bring binoculars if you have them. What do you see in the sky? You may see stars and planets. (Stars twinkle, but planets do not.) Do you see any strange or moving lights? What could those be?

LOOK AT ALL THE STARS AND STRANGE LIGHTS!

GLOSSARY

PLANETS bodies that move around a star

SCIENTISTS people who study how the world works

SCI-FI stories about science, space, or technology; short for "science fiction"

TELESCOPES objects used to see things far away

UFOS unidentified flying objects; also called "flying saucers"

WEATHER BALLOON a large balloon that gathers information about the weather

READ MORE

Erickson, Justin. *Alien Abductions*. Minneapolis: Bellwether Media, 2011.

Wencel, Dave. *UFOs*. Minneapolis: Bellwether Media, 2011.

INDEX

WEBSITES

Do Aliens Really Exist?
http://discoverykids.com/articles/do-aliens-really-exist/
Learn more about aliens and UFOs.

It Came from Outer Space
http://lifestyle.howstuffworks.com/crafts/quick-easy-crafts/easy-outdoor-science
-experiments-for-kids6.htm
Try out a fun science experiment about space.

Note: Every effort has been made to ensure that the websites listed above are suitable for children, that they have educational value, and that they contain no inappropriate material. However, because of the nature of the Internet, it is impossible to guarantee that these sites will remain active indefinitely or that their contents will not be altered.